JOAN TOWER

SECOND STRING FORCE

FOR SOLO VIOLIN

AMP 8319

First Printing: December 2017

ISBN: 978-1-4950-9927-4

Associated Music Publishers, Inc.

DISTRIBUTED BY

HAL•LEONARD®

www.halleonard.com

www.musicsalesclassical.com

Commissioned with the generous support of
Elizabeth Serkin and Herman Silverman

First performance: 16 March 2015
Bella Hristova, violin
Merkin Concert Hall
New York, NY

Composer Note:

SECOND STRING FORCE is dedicated to my friend and brilliant violinist Bella Hristova who premiered the work in New York City at Merkin Concert Hall, sponsored by Young Concert Artists.

This work follows another solo violin piece – STRING FORCE – which was commissioned by the International Violin Competition of Indianapolis in 2010. That work is dedicated to Bella's teacher and mentor, the wonderful violinist/conductor Jaime Laredo, hence the title SECOND STRING FORCE.

In both of these works, I tried to show the "force" of a solo violin – both in terms of its capacity for high and fast energy as well as its deep lyrical-melodic capabilities, particularly how it can play very softly in the highest register.

There is a beautiful performance of this piece on YouTube by Bella.

— Joan Tower

duration circa 8 minutes, 30 seconds

Information on Joan Tower and her works is available on musicsalesclassical.com

to Bella Hristova
commissioned with the generous support of Elizabeth Serkin and Herman Silverman

SECOND STRING FORCE

Joan Tower

Poco più mosso ♪ = ca. 120

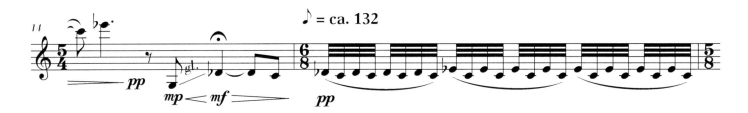

♪ = ca. 132

♩ = ca. 52

broaden

♪ = ca. 132

♩ = ca. 120

cresc. poco a poco

(cresc.)   p   cresc. poco a poco

poco a poco to ord.

(cresc.)   mp   cresc.

ord.

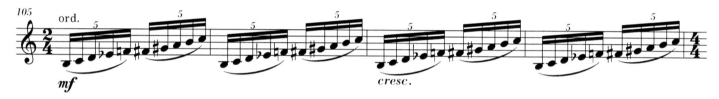

mf   cresc.

f

mf   legato   cresc.

(cresc.)   f

cresc.

ff

Poco più mosso